OLIVER AND THE TWINS

(An adaptation of the book by the same title by Amy Lefeuvre.
Permission granted by Lutterworth Press, London, England.)

Adapted by: Rose Mae Carvin

Art Work by: Mrs. John Hertzler

Introduction

When our Lord Jesus Christ was living on this earth, He taught a great deal — including how to pray.

One day on a mountainside, many people sat listening to Him. "When you pray," He said, "use not vain repetitions, as the heathen do: for they think that they shall be heard for their much speaking. Be not ye therefore like unto them: for your Father knoweth what things ye have need of, before ye ask Him. After this manner therefore pray ye" (Matthew 6:7, 8).

Then the Lord Jesus taught His listeners, and us, what we call "The Lord's Prayer." It is this prayer about which we shall be hearing in our story of Oliver and his twin sisters. In the beginning of our story they *said* the Lord's Prayer, not really understanding what it meant. I am afraid they were doing what the Lord Jesus said we are not to do, using "vain repetitions." But at the end of the story—well, you will find out! Let's begin with . . .

CHAPTER ONE

"Our Father Which Art in Heaven"

1

Oliver was fifteen years old, but he felt much older. He stood leaning on the white gate which was at the end of the lane leading to a little cottage in England.

The cottage was empty now. It had been the home of Oliver and his twin sisters ever since his father died. Here it was that his mother had cared for her children as best she could, selling her paintings to keep Oliver in school. Oliver loved the cottage. He remembered many happy days spent there.

Everything was changed now, however. Tears came to Oliver's eyes as he remembered the day his mother died, only a week before. "My son," she had said, "there is no one to care for the girls now except you. You will have to leave school for a time, but I trust for not too long.

"You have heard me speak of my brother who, because he was displeased about my marrying your dear father, never came to see me after we were married. I do not know where he lives now. But I have heard he moved to Topminster. I want you to take the girls and try to find him there. He will give you advice on what to do, I know. You can find work easier in the city than here in the country.

2

"And, Oliver, my boy, I know I am putting a heavy burden on your shoulders. But I want you to promise me that you will rear the girls properly. Above all I want you to teach them

to love God. I know they, as well as you, Oliver, are Christians. I remember well when each of you took the Lord Jesus into your heart. God will look after you, because He is your Father."

Oliver had quickly promised his mother to care for his sisters. But now, as he leaned on the little white gate, he wondered if he would be able to keep those promises. *How is a fifteen-year-old boy going to be able to care for two lively seven-year-old girls?* he thought. *But I do not have to do it alone. Even if we never find our uncle, God is our Father and He will lead me.* Oliver squared his shoulders, held his dark head high, and walked away, his eyes shining with determination.

He and the girls had been staying with a kind neighbor down the road after everything was sold out of the cottage. Tomorrow he planned to leave, with the twins, for Topminster where he hoped to find his uncle. That night, after the girls were in bed, shining blond curls spread out on their pillows and blue eyes closed in sweet sleep, Oliver and the neighbor had a long talk.

"Where will you stay until you find your uncle?" the neighbor asked.

"I do not know. But God is our Father and He knows. I am trusting Him to show me what to do." Oliver spoke with confidence.

"Well then, God has put it into my mind to send you to my sister. Topminster is a big place and you may not find your uncle right away. You give my sister this note and I am sure she will let you stay with her for a while."

Oliver thanked the neighbor and went to bed with a lighter heart.

3

The twins were quite excited the next day as they boarded the train which would carry them to a strange new world. As they sat looking out the window and chattering away, Oliver did some thinking about finances.

His mother had left a little money in the bank. But Oliver knew it would not last long in a big city. He was taking his mother's painting tools with him. Perhaps he would be able to paint well enough to sell—at least for a while. His mother had taught him to paint and he knew that his sketches were fairly good. In his arms he carried one of his mother's paintings. It was the last one she had done. She had told Oliver it was a picture of her home where she lived when she was a girl. Oliver purposed never to part with it.

When the train pulled into the station at Topminster, the girls were frightened by the crowds. "What's happened?" asked Babs. "Is it a funeral? Or a circus? Or is the queen going by?"

"Let us wait until all these people go before we leave!" Debbie exclaimed, holding Oliver's hand tightly.

Oliver laughed. "You have never been in a big city before," he said. "There will always be lots of people around everywhere. Come, let's get a cab."

The neighbor's sister welcomed the brave young man and his lively sisters. "I am rather crowded with roomers," she said. "But if you do not mind a room on the top floor, there is one there that will do for the girls. Next to it there is a small dressing room which you could use for yourself."

Oliver and his sisters climbed two flights of stairs and were grateful for the little rooms and for the supper the landlady sent up to them. When they were ready for bed Oliver said, "Let us say our prayers together tonight and end with the Lord's Prayer."

4

"Oh, that's what everybody says," Babs objected. "I expect God gets very tired of hearing it. *I'm* tired of it. And I don't understand it. Neither does Debbie."

"No, neither do I," Debbie echoed. She almost always followed Babs in everything.

"Well first," Oliver said, "it tells us that God is our Father when we trust in Him and belong to Him. He is our Father because we have received His Son, the Lord Jesus, as our Saviour. Now He is living in our hearts."

"Yes, we remember when we knelt with Mommy at home and asked the Lord Jesus to be our Saviour, don't we, Debbie?"

Debbie nodded her head.

"Well then, we can say 'Our Father' and really mean it," Oliver said. "And if He is our Father He will look after us. He will show us what to do. I am sure God does not get tired of hearing us say 'Our Father, which art in heaven' when we really mean it.

"Each night we shall talk a little more about the Lord's Prayer. We can have our quiet time together. Would you like that?"

Sleepily the girls nodded their heads. Together they said the Lord's Prayer, exactly as the Lord Jesus taught it to His disciples (Matthew 6:9-13). Oliver kissed them good night and tucked them in. Soon they were sound asleep dreaming of the great adventure of the past day.

5

Oliver went downstairs to talk to the landlady. He asked to see a city directory and turned to the SMITH column. His heart sank. There were a great many Smiths and a surprisingly long line of J. Smiths! His uncle's name was J. Smith. This was all Oliver knew.

"I'll simply have to call on every one of these J. Smiths," he said, "and hope I'll not have to go too far before I find the right one. Meanwhile the first thing I must do is to find a job."

The landlady said she would be willing for the girls to stay with her while Oliver was out. "They can play in the park down the street," she said. "They will love it there."

Oliver was a little troubled about the girls being left alone in a park in a strange city. *But what else can I do?* he thought. *Anyhow I must not forget that our Father will be watching over them.*

CHAPTER TWO
"Hallowed Be Thy Name"

When Oliver returned to his room the next evening he was discouraged because he had not been able to get in touch with any of the J. Smiths. But he was happy about having found work. It was not a very good job and did not pay much. But it was work and he would at least be able to buy food.

6

The girls were all excited. "We found a friend in the park, Oliver!" Babs exclaimed. "And guess what! She lives right in this house. She talked to us and asked us if our father were dead. We said, 'Oh no, Ma'am. He isn't dead. He looks after us and after Mommy, too. Only Mommy doesn't live with us. She lives in heaven. Our Father is God.' "

Debbie added, "Then the lady said, 'Oh, I see,' in such a funny way, Oliver."

"She told us her name is Miss Gregory and we told her ours," Babs explained. "I said, 'I am Barbara Coventry and this is my sister—my twin sister—Deborah Coventry. And our brother is Oliver Coventry.' We asked her if she knew our Father and she said she did. We are going to visit her in her rooms some day and have a little party, if you say we may, Oliver."

"Yes, of course you may, if she lives here," Oliver said. "I shall have to leave you alone most of the time. Promise you will be very quiet and not disturb anyone. We don't want our landlady to make us move before we find our uncle, do we?"

"Oh, we'll be good, Oliver," Babs said, "won't we, Debbie?"

"Oh yes, we'll be so good you will hardly know us, Oliver."

"Well, I surely hope so." Oliver smiled at their eagerness. He knew they would try. How successful they would be, he was not certain. Oliver knew the girls needed to go to school. But in England even going to public school costs money. And he did not see how he would be able to send them. He prayed, "Our Father, You know of this need. Please show me what to do."

7

The answer to Oliver's prayer was not long in coming. The very next evening Miss Gregory came to their rooms for a talk. "I have been a teacher in a girls' school," she said. "But because of my health I have had to give it up. I would consider it a favor to me if you would allow me to keep in practice by teaching your sisters. I would expect no pay."

Oliver thanked Miss Gregory even as his heart whispered, "Thank You, my Father. Thank You so much."

The little girls were disappointed at first because they were to stay in each morning and study. But they soon learned to love Miss Gregory and she made their studies seem like fun to them. Added to their regular school work she gave them some lessons on the Bible. She made *Quiet Time Notebooks* for each one. "Each night before you say your prayers and go to bed, please get Oliver to help you to answer these questions," she said. "You really ought to get to know about this Book which our Father has written because He has written it to His children. And you are His children."

Miss Gregory was not the only friend the girls made in the park where they went each afternoon. An old man came there each day to sweep the walks and gather up the fallen leaves. He always sat on a bench to eat his lunch. It was there the girls found him.

8

"How do you do?" Babs said politely. "My name is Barbara and this is my twin sister Deborah. Would you like us to sweep up some leaves for you while you eat your lunch?"

"Well now!" the old man exclaimed, his mouth full of bread. "My name is Amos and I'd appreciate it very much if you would help me with the leaves."

Each day after that the girls watched for Amos when they went to the park to play. He always had some special treat in his lunch box for them and they helped him with his sweeping. Then he would tell them stories. They liked Amos very much and the funny words he used made them laugh.

9

The twins told their brother about Amos. He did not object to their friendship until one day he heard Babs say, "Lord-a-mercy, Debbie, you've spilled jelly on your dress."

"Who taught you to say *that*?" Oliver demanded.

"Oh, Amos says it. I think it sounds very nice! He says a lot of funny words."

"Then he is not fit company for you!" Oliver exclaimed.

"He's very good, Amos is," Debbie said. "He is always calling out God's name when he works."

"That is *swearing*," Oliver said. "It is wicked to say God's name when you mean nothing by it. It's what the commandment says we're not to do—not to take God's name in vain. We are not to speak His name for nothing."

The twins stared at their brother.

"Is it wicked to say, 'By God, I'll give it to him'?"

"Very wicked!"

Babs looked at Debbie with sorrowful eyes. "Amos must be a very wicked man." Both girls started to cry.

"And we liked him so much," Debbie sobbed. "He tells such nice stories."

Quiet Time Notebooks are small colored folders with insert sheets for each month, to help boys and girls in their private devotions. Further information about these Quiet Time Notebooks may be obtained from the publisher.

That night as Oliver and the twins had their quiet time together, Oliver tried to explain about the sin of swearing.

"You have learned what we mean when we say, 'Our Father.' We know we belong to Him and He is watching over us. Now let us learn a little about the meaning of the next part of the Lord's Prayer. Do you know what 'Hallowed be Thy name' means?"

Both girls shook their heads.

"It means that God's name must be kept holy. Holy things are not to be talked about in a loud voice or shouted in the streets. If people love God they are reverent and careful in the way they talk about Him. You say 'Hallowed be Thy name' and you must 'hallow' it yourself and get others to do the same."

"Yes, we will," Babs said. "We'll tell Amos he must not use God's name like he does."

Good as her word, the very next time the girls saw Amos, Babs exclaimed, "Oliver thinks you are wicked!"

The old man looked angry. "Oh, he does, does he? Well let him come here and tell me that to my face! I'll give that young smarty a good licking. That's what I'll do."

"Well, Amos, you see," Debbie said, "it's about our prayer. Do you know how to 'hallow,' Amos?"

Without waiting for the old man to reply she continued, "Isn't it a funny word? It means we must speak God's name softly and lovingly because He is our Father. And you just shout it all over the place, Amos. That is being wicked. When you say 'Lord-a-mercy' it sounds like the name doesn't belong to God at all. Oliver says that *Lord* is one of God's names. So we must have respect when we use it—like in a prayer."

10

Amos forgot his anger as he looked into the sweet faces of the girls. "Bless your hearts," he said. "I never meant any harm. I meant nothing at all by those words."

Babs was relieved. "Well we didn't want you to be wicked, Amos. I guess if you didn't mean anything wrong and will try not to swear any more it will be all right. You won't do it ever again, will you? Oliver says God is our Father and we mustn't let our Father's name be called out in the streets or made fun of."

One night, some time later, after they had finished the work in their Quiet Time Notebooks and were ready for prayer, Babs said, "God's Name is quite 'hallowed' in the park now, Oliver. Amos never even whispers it. He isn't wicked any more."

"I am glad to hear he has stopped swearing," Oliver said. "But there is lots of wickedness in the world besides that. We are just as bad as Amos, I am certain.

"God tells us in His Word that everyone has sinned (Romans 3:23). Because of our sin all of us deserve to be punished. So even though Amos has stopped swearing he still has sin in his heart. God tells us that there is only one way to escape this punishment, and that is to receive His Son, the Lord Jesus. Babs, do you remember the verse you memorized when you asked the Lord Jesus to come into your heart and forgive your sin?"

"Oh, yes." she replied, with a big smile on her face. "It is John 14:6, 'I am the Way, the Truth, and the Life: no man cometh unto the Father, but by Me.' "

"That's right," said Oliver. "And don't you think that our Father wants Amos to know how to come to Him? Don't *you* want your friend, Amos, to know the way to heaven?"

Babs and Debbie were ashamed that they had not witnessed to Amos about the Lord Jesus. "We shall be sure to tell him tomorrow," they agreed. "And we shall pray for Amos each night, too."

"Well, there is one thing," Debbie said, "we know now what 'hallow' means when we pray the Lord's Prayer. I used to think it was the same as a hollow tree."

Oliver shook his head as he laughed. How was he ever going to do the right thing for these sisters of his? He was very grateful for Miss Gregory and for the lessons she gave the girls on the Bible. He, too, was learning a great deal at their quiet time. They all looked forward to these times together.

CHAPTER THREE

"Thy Kingdom Come"

Oliver kept trying to find their uncle. Week after week after week he tried. But always without success. It was a bright sunny Saturday when he said to the twins, "This afternoon we shall have a trip into the country. There is a Mr. J. Smith who moved out there from Topminster. He is the last of the J. Smiths. If he is not our uncle, I'll have to give up."

Of course the twins were delighted with the prospect of a trip to the country. The park was the closest thing they had seen to the country since they left home. They clapped their hands and scurried about getting ready.

11

After the long bus ride they had an even longer walk to the big house. The girls were almost worn out. "Are we nearly there, Oliver?" Debbie asked softly.

"Yes, Debbie, nearly there. It is just over this hill." He put his arms around the girls trying to help them along as best he could. "Just think how wonderful it will be if this turns out to be our uncle."

"Well, let's hope he is a kind man, if he is our uncle," Babs said in a tired little voice.

"Look, there it is!" Oliver exclaimed as they reached the top of the hill. "See the name, 'Elmhurst'? This is the place."

Oliver was nervous as he passed through the big gates and walked up the winding path to the big house. But the twins straightened their shoulders and held their blond heads high. No uncle was going to scare them.

"Perhaps I should have written a letter first," Oliver said. "Maybe we shouldn't have come out like this."

"Now don't you worry, Oliver. You know our Father in heaven is watching over us and we need not be afraid of anyone." Babs reached up and patted her brother's cheek.

"That's right, Oliver," Debbie chimed in, "not a single, teensy, weensy, little bit afraid."

12

Oliver squared his shoulders again and rang the doorbell. A footman opened the heavy door, "Yes?" he said, raising his eyebrows when he saw the tired children.

"May I speak to Mr. Smith?" Oliver was trying to keep his voice steady.

"Mr. Smith is not at home."

"May I speak to Mrs. Smith then?"

"Mrs. Smith is busy with guests and cannot be disturbed." The butler was just about to close the door again when a woman came down the long hall. Oliver's heart raced as he stepped forward.

"If you are Mrs. Smith I'd like very much to speak to you for a moment," he said bravely. "We have walked a long way and it is very important."

The woman frowned. "I have guests this afternoon but if you can say what you have to say in a few minutes, come with me." She led Oliver into one of the many rooms. The butler motioned for the girls to sit down in a big chair in the hall.

13

Babs and Debbie sat together very straight. They were frightened themselves now. Many people came in and out from the rooms close by. But none spoke to the girls until a little lady with a sweet face and snow-white hair came down the long flight of stairs. She smiled as she saw the girls.

"What a pretty picture you make sitting there looking exactly alike," she said. "Please sit still while I get my camera." Soon she was back and click, she had their picture before they knew what was happening!

"You poor dears look so tired," the lady said. "Do you mind telling me what you are doing here sitting so still in this big hall?"

The girls spoke politely and told the lady their names and where they lived and why they were in the hall waiting for their brother.

The lady smiled. "My name is Mrs. Sutherland," she said. They loved her smile and noticed how kind her eyes were. "Come with me," she said, "and I'll get you something to drink. Perhaps you'd like to hear some music while you wait."

Following the woman into one of the many rooms, the girls sipped cool lemonade while the lady played the piano and sang. The song was very sad, they thought. It was about a little girl who had died. They were glad that the song said that the little girl had gone to heaven. Heaven was a kingdom, the song said. No one ever died there. They were glad to listen to the song but it reminded them of their mother who lived in heaven and before long they were telling Mrs. Sutherland all about themselves.

14

When they heard the angry voice of Mrs. Smith in the hall, the girls went out quickly. "Young man," she was saying, "be sure you are on the right track before you bother strangers like this again!"

Oliver took hold of the hands of his sisters and walked to the door. Turning, he said, "I have apologized to you, Mrs. Smith. I can do no more."

Walking back, the way seemed even longer because of the disappointment in their hearts. "I have to give up now," Oliver said. "We must make up our minds to do without an uncle. At least I have done as I promised I'd do."

"We've got God left," Debbie whispered.

Oliver smiled. "Yes, I haven't forgotten. We'll pull through all right."

All the way home the twins talked about Mrs. Sutherland and the little song. "The kingdom, in the song, means heaven, Oliver. That's where no flowers or anything else ever dies. What is a kingdom, Oliver?"

"Well, a kingdom is a country which belongs to a king or queen. The English (or British) kingdom belongs to our queen. Those who live in a kingdom are the subjects of the king or queen."

"And the kingdom with the beautiful garden is heaven, isn't it?" Babs asked. "Is it the same as 'kingdom come' in 'Our Father which art in heaven?' Is God the King?"

"Yes," Oliver answered. "God's kingdom is going to be on this earth some day. That's why we pray for it to come. God is really King of the world now. But His kingdom isn't seen. It is inside the hearts of people who believe in Him. They are His subjects and should do His will. When you are children of His kingdom, you serve Him and please Him. Some day the Lord Jesus Christ will come to the world again and rule as King. Then it will be His kingdom."

"We want the kingdom to come, don't we, Debbie?"

Debbie replied, "Oh yes, we want it very much."

And that night, after quiet time, two little sleepy heads bowed as they repeated "Thy kingdom come," in a new way.

Hugging Oliver, Babs exclaimed, "Oh, Oliver, we're so glad we have a brother like you! I'm glad we did not find our uncle today, if he was going to be cross like his wife was."

"Yes," Debbie said, "but Mrs. Sutherland was nice. And she said she is going to come to see us some day."

That "some day" came very soon. One evening when Oliver got home from work he found her there having a visit with the twins. Eagerly they showed him the presents she had brought them.

"I have fallen in love with your sisters, young man, and I'd like to know you, also. Will you come to see me some day?"

15

Standing before his mother's painting, Mrs. Sutherland added, "If you ever want to sell this, I hope you'll give me first chance. I'd like very much to buy it."

"It is the only painting I have of my mother's and I shall never part with it—unless I really have to," Oliver said. "But I thank you very much. We'll look forward to a visit with you in your home."

When Mrs. Sutherland left, Oliver knew they had found a friend in the gentle woman. *This is perhaps why God led me to go to the country after all,* he thought. *Not to find an uncle—but to find a friend.*

CHAPTER FOUR

"Thy Will Be Done"

There came a day which Oliver said afterward seemed to have in it nothing but trouble.

The twins were not to have lessons with Miss Gregory in the morning because she was away for the day. And because it was a cold winter day, Oliver told them not to go to the park until early afternoon when the sun would be warmer.

"We won't mind as long as the landlady lets us play with her kitten," Babs said. "She said we might."

16

Everything had gone along smoothly until the twins began chasing the kitten around the room. When the kitten jumped on the table to get away from them, it knocked over a big pitcher. The pitcher fell to the floor, smashed into many pieces, spilling water all over the girls' coats on a nearby chair.

As the girls stood there, frightened, the landlady hurried to their room. "What was that crash?" she demanded. The twins said nothing. Nor did they need to, for the landlady saw at once what had happened.

"You are naughty girls," she said, shaking Debbie. "Just look what you have done to my pitcher! And you've got your coats all wet! Now you cannot go to the park at all today."

When Babs saw the landlady shaking her sister she was angry. "You leave my sister alone," she screamed, "or I'll hit you—hard!"

Debbie squirmed away from the landlady. "We shall too go to the park!" she yelled.

Babs started to cry. She was usually a sweet little thing. But she could not stand to see her sister hurt in any way. "It was an accident and it was all your old kitten's fault anyhow. You have no right to scold us and we'll tell our brother when he gets home. Wait until he finds out you shook Debbie."

"Well, I never!" the angry landlady shouted. "You two and your brother will leave my house at once. I'll not have such impudent girls as you are living in my house. And don't you dare leave this room for the rest of the day." Slam! went the door as the landlady rushed out. The windows shook.

17

Debbie looked at Babs with wide, frightened eyes. "Whatever shall we do now?" she wailed.

"Do? We'll just go on out and see Amos. That's what we'll do!"

"But we can't go out. Our coats are soaking wet."

"We'll hang them by the fire to dry and leave them here. Come on, put this warm cap on. We won't freeze."

The girls crept softly down the stairs and out the door. "Now keep running," Babs instructed. "That will keep you warm."

The girls were chilled clear through when they got to the little shack where Amos ate his lunch in cold weather. He was surprised to see them without their coats.

18

Between them Babs and Debbie told Amos the whole story. They thought he would sympathize with them and were surprised when he said, "Now, you see here! You are the little girls who told me I was a wicked man because I took God's name in vain. You taught me the Lord's Prayer and what it means to hallow God's Name. Best of all you told me about the Lord Jesus. And now that I have received Him, some day I can go to heaven."

"Yes, Amos, and we're glad. But what has this to do with what we just told you?"

"It's got this to do with it," Amos said sternly. "Part of the Lord's Prayer says 'Thy will be done on earth as it is in heaven.' "

"That's right, but Oliver hasn't explained that to us yet."

"Well, it seems to me you girls have been doing Satan's will this day. Sure, the broken pitcher was an accident. But if you hadn't been playing rough with the kitten in a small room, it would not have happened. And to speak as you did to your landlady and to run out without coats when she told you not to go out—well this certainly is not doing God's will as the angels in heaven do His will. Now you go right straight home! Run, mind you, before you catch your death of cold. And you tell that landlady you're sorry for speaking to her as you did."

"Nobody is kind to us today," the twins pouted as they ran home.

19

When they got close to their room they could smell something burning. It was their coats! And they were burned nearly to pieces. They had hung them too close to the fire. And, where the coats had fallen to the floor, there was a hole burned in the little rug. Frightened, the girls stomped on the rug and put out the fire.

Poor Oliver, arriving home tired after a hard day's work, just sat and stared for a few moments when he heard all that had happened.

"At first we hid the burnt coats under the bed, Oliver. But then we knew you'd find out anyhow. So we took them out again. Amos says we have been doing the devil's will this day. Do you say so, too, Oliver?"

"Well, you certainly haven't been doing the Lord's will," Oliver said. "I think I agree with Amos. Off to bed with you both! Right away! Tomorrow you stay there all day as a punishment. But wait. First you must go downstairs and tell the landlady you're sorry you spoke to her as you did."

When they were back in their room Debbie looked at Oliver, tears in her eyes. "Amos says the angels do God's will. You know, Oliver. 'Thy will be done on earth as it is in heaven.' Do you think angels go to bed, Oliver?"

Oliver looked puzzled. "No, I don't suppose angels go to bed. Why do you ask?"

"Well, if angels don't go to bed, why must we? We promise to do God's will on earth from now on, Oliver. Must we stay in bed tomorrow?"

On the next day there was no question about the girls' staying in bed. They were sick with heavy colds and had to have the doctor come in.

That night Oliver knelt beside the bed where the girls lay sniffing. "I'll pray for us all tonight, girls," he said. "But please pay attention." The girls stopped their crying as Oliver read the Bible to them. He allowed them to sit up and try to do some work in their Quiet Time Notebooks. Then Oliver prayed earnestly for God to help them to be good girls and do His will.

The landlady was really angry about the burnt rug. Even when the little girls said they were sorry, she did not forgive them. She told Oliver he would have to find another place as soon as possible.

Oliver sat for a long time beside the fire that night. How he longed for his mother. He would have to pay for the pitcher and the rug. He had a doctor to pay now and the medicine had cost a great deal more than he could afford. And coats! The girls would have to have new winter coats immediately.

Oliver lifted his head and looked long and lovingly at his mother's painting. He would have to sell it. The money in the bank was all gone and he could not make enough to pay for these things.

The next day Oliver asked Miss Gregory to sit with the twins for awhile. As he went out he carried his mother's painting in his arms. He would take it to Mrs. Sutherland. She had asked to buy it.

But Mrs. Sutherland was not at home. She would not be back for a week. Disappointed, Oliver turned his steps toward the store where he knew paintings were on sale.

20

The shopkeeper told Oliver the painting was worth more than he could afford to pay for it. But Oliver said he had to have money right away and was willing to take whatever he could give him.

"Well, laddie, if I sell it for a good deal more I shall share the profit with you. I wish I could give you more."

Again, at bedtime, he and the girls had their quiet time together. They understood now so well what, "Our Father which art in heaven" meant. And they certainly knew also that because God was their kind Father who cared for them, they ought always to do His will on earth even as the angels in heaven do His will there.

Surely their heavenly Father looked down lovingly on these children who had no parents.

CHAPTER FIVE

"Give Us This Day Our Daily Bread"

21

When Miss Gregory learned that Oliver and the twins needed a new place to live, she had a suggestion.

"I have a friend who lives only a little way outside the city," she said. "Her husband used to be the head gardener for a big house out there. When he died, the owners allowed her to stay on in the gardener's cottage. She lives alone and might be glad for company. But you would have the extra distance to travel to and from your work, Oliver."

"It would be so good to live in the country again," Oliver said. "I'd be willing to travel the extra distance. I've been very worried about the twins, alone here in a big city so much. Will you please ask your friend if we may talk to her about rooms?"

Word came that the gardener's wife was willing to see them. So the next Saturday afternoon when Oliver was free, he took his little sisters out to see her. They felt proud in the new warm coats Oliver had bought them.

The cottage was small but the gardener's wife said they could have a tiny room for the girls, if Oliver was willing to sleep in a big chair which opened into a single bed. The chair-bed was in a tiny room at the end of the hall.

Oliver was grateful for this answer to prayer. The twins were quite excited at the prospect of playing in the woods close by.

The night before they were to leave their old place, Miss Gregory came to their rooms for a visit. She brought two lovely hand-knit dresses for the girls. They squealed with delight.

"We're rich! First, new coats and now, new dresses!"

"What a lot of kind people there are in the world!" Oliver's eyes filled with tears. "Thank you so very much, Miss Gregory. We hope you'll come to see us often. The girls will miss you."

"Perhaps," Miss Gregory replied.

When Oliver looked surprised she said, "I have a plan. The road to your new home is a quiet one and I am sure the girls would be safe walking on it alone. Could you bring them to me when you go to work, Oliver? Then in the afternoon I could take them out of the city and see them safely on the road back home. This way they could continue their lessons."

"Oh, Miss Gregory, this has been bothering me a great deal—about their lessons, I mean. I did not see how they were to continue their studies. But I knew our Father would show me a way when it was His time. You have been a real friend and we are very grateful."

At first the girls were a little disappointed. They loved Miss Gregory. But secretly they had been happy when they thought they would not need to study any more.

* * * * *

All else was forgotten but the beauty of the country and the many new things to see at their new home when they arrived the next day.

22

The gardener's cottage where they were now to live, was much like their cottage where they had lived with their mother. To Oliver it brought back many happy memories.

Up the long, narrow stairway they climbed, each carrying a piece of luggage. There was just one window in the girls' room. But it faced towards the woods, much to the delight of Babs and Debbie.

"We may see foxes creeping down through the woods."

"And dear little rabbits."

"But when it's dark there may be robbers hiding there!"

"Wouldn't it be fun to see them creeping under the trees?"

"I don't know. I'd rather see some fairies dancing."

"We'll play out there every afternoon when the weather is nice."

"That will be lovely."

Oliver turned to their new landlady. "Would we be trespassing if we walked in the woods a little before dark?"

"Bless you, no! The family from the big house is away. If you meet any of the servants just tell them you are staying at my house and it will be all right."

Up a steep hill they climbed. At the top they could see miles away in each direction. The sun was beginning to set. It sent pale lemon colors, streaked with gray, into the sky. Slowly the sky turned to a soft pink.

"Oh, what sunsets I shall paint from here!" Oliver exclaimed. "I may even be able to sell some of them for a good price."

As they turned to go back to the cottage, Oliver noticed two fat little faces looking out at them from the bushes.

"Hello," Oliver said, "who are you, please?"

23

The owners of the fat faces, a boy and a girl, did not answer Oliver. Instead they made ugly faces at him and the twins and then they ran down the hill. Half way down they stopped and yelled, imitating Oliver, "Hello, who are you, please? Ha! Never mind who we are. We want to know, who are *you*? And we don't want you here! So go on home." With that they took off again.

"I wonder who those mean children are?" Babs asked.

"They may belong to one of the servants at the big house. Pay no attention to them and they will probably leave you alone."

That night Oliver and the girls sat doing the work in their Quiet Time Notebooks. As usual they ended their individual prayers by repeating the Lord's Prayer together. When they got to "give us this day our daily bread," Oliver stopped them. "We'll say that part over again, and really mean it when we say it."

The girls raised their heads. "Why, Oliver?"

"Because I want you to know our daily bread is not easy to get right now. I don't know how long our money will hold out. We must ask God with all our hearts to give it to us. He hasn't failed us yet. But I'm in a tight fix now. I want you to pray often, 'give us this day our daily bread!' "

"Perhaps," suggested Debbie, "sweet rolls would be cheaper than bread. We'd like them just as well."

Oliver shook his head. "Let us finish our prayer," he said.

Before they got into bed Babs said, "I suppose the Lord Jesus prayed that because He and His disciples were starving hungry sometimes. They were very poor, weren't they? And you told us that the Lord Jesus taught His disciples the Lord's Prayer."

"Yes, they were often hungry, I'm sure," Oliver said. "And I know we shall be taken care of. But we must pray, for the Lord Jesus told us to do so."

24

The next Saturday afternoon the new landlady took Oliver and the girls all through the lovely gardens which belonged to the owner of the big house. They saw hothouses, water and rock gardens, a rose garden, and beautiful terraces. "Wait until you see the roses in bloom," the landlady said.

The place the twins liked best was known as the children's garden. It was enclosed by old stone walls. A swing, a tiny summerhouse and low seats were there. In the center of the garden was a thatched pigeon house. Pigeons strutted up and down the wall.

The girls saw some rabbit hutches and a squirrel's cage. These were empty now. "There are no children living in the big house now," the landlady said.

As they were walking back towards the cottage, they saw the same two fat faces peering out from the bushes making faces at them. "They are the cook's children," the landlady explained. "They are mean. Try to pay no attention to them."

25

When they got back to the cottage a visitor was waiting for them. It was their friend, Mrs. Sutherland. She told Oliver she was sorry to have been away when he called. She was most disappointed when she discovered that Oliver had sold his mother's picture.

"I have some good news for you, Oliver," she said, "A friend of mine is a banker. He needs a clerk and I have recommended you. Your pay will be twice as much as you are getting now."

That night at quiet time, Oliver prayed, "Thank You, our Father, for answering our prayers. Thank You for supplying our daily bread."

"And sometimes sweet rolls, too," Debbie added.

Within a week Oliver was working at the bank.

CHAPTER SIX

"Forgive Us Our Trespasses As We Forgive Those Who Trespass Against Us"

Ever since the twins had seen the children's garden, when their new landlady had taken them through the gardens, they planned one of their own.

"It will be a doll's garden," Debbie said.

"Well, I think it will be for elves and little brownies. They always live in the woods."

The garden began to develop into a thing of real beauty. The girls were proud of it and spent most of their free time there. Oliver made them a tiny gate and a wheelbarrow, exactly the right size for the garden.

There came a week when it rained each day. The girls grew restless. When Oliver learned that the landlady was to be away one whole day, he was worried. *Would the twins get into mischief?* he wondered.

As he left for work, Oliver said, "I do not want you in my room today—not for anything. Understand? Not for *anything!*"

"But why, Oliver?" Babs wanted to know.

"It would be so nice to think you would obey me without knowing all the reasons for my orders," Oliver said. "But I'll tell you. I have been painting in the morning before I go to work. Because of the rain, the sketch is quite wet this morning. I have stood it on my dresser to dry and I don't want anything to happen to it. I have an order for it at a good price."

26

The twins amused themselves for awhile by playing in their tiny room and the hall outside. But knowing there was no one to stop them, they began running all over the cottage. Up and down the stairs they went—in and out of rooms, chasing each other.

Babs forgot what Oliver had said about his room and she opened the door and dashed in there. Debbie followed. They jumped over the chair-bed. Babs grabbed a pillow and threw it at Debbie. It landed on the dresser where Oliver's sketch stood.

"Oh, look, Debbie, the sun has come out!" Babs yelled as she opened the window to look out. Neither girl observed Oliver's sketch which slid slowly down and blew out the window.

Out to their little garden they ran. The earth was nice and soft after the rain. So they pulled weeds until they were tired. "These nasty things try to choke out our flowers," they said. They did not notice the fat, round faces peering out at them as they worked.

"Let's get back to the house and clean off some of this mud," Babs said, "before the landlady gets back."

Close to the house they discovered Oliver's sketch, all wet and muddy. They looked at each other realizing what had happened. "We forgot to close the window," Debbie said in a scared voice.

Babs picked up the sketch and tried to wipe it on her dress. Of course the paint smeared, both on the sketch and on her dress.

"Now what are we going to do?" Debbie wailed.

"Let's take it to the fire and dry it off."

Before long the sketch had a scorched spot in one corner.

Debbie began to cry. "We're always doing something wrong."

"Let's not tell Oliver anything about it," Babs suggested.

"It's your fault, Babs," Debbie accused. "You were the one to open Oliver's door and go into his room first. And you opened the window."

27

"Well you went in, too! You're just as bad. Come on. Let's hide it behind the bushes outside and let him find it himself."

When Oliver came home the girls lied to him, just as they had planned.

"I cannot trust you," Oliver said. "You promised you would not go into my room and you did. Now I wonder if you are telling me the truth. You don't look as though you are."

"Perhaps," said Debbie timidly, "the sketch blew out the window. It was open when we were in there."

"And I know I left the window closed so my sketch would dry. You opened it, didn't you? And the sketch blew out." The girls cried softly as Oliver went outside and came in with what was left of his sketch.

Oliver's heart was heavy. How he longed for his mother again! She would know how to handle a thing like this. He was disappointed about the picture for he was sure he could have sold it. That very day the man in the shop had called him in and given him more money for his mother's painting. A gentleman had been interested in the picture and had paid a good price for it. The shopkeeper wanted some of Oliver's paintings to sell. But Oliver's worst disappointment was knowing that the twins had been naughty.

Before they did the work in their notebooks and had prayer together, the girls told Oliver the whole story of what had happened to his sketch.

28

"Please, Oliver, forgive us," Debbie begged. "We never meant to ruin your sketch. And we are terribly sorry about it, aren't we, Babs?"

Babs choked back a sob. "Oliver, please do forgive us. But I have to tell you it was really *my* fault. I went into your room first and you know Debbie always follows whatever I do. So if you can't forgive us both, please, Oliver, forgive Debbie. I expect you just can't forgive us both."

Oliver felt a lump in his throat. He loved these little sisters very much. "Of course I forgive you. I forgive you both. But I am disappointed. To do a wrong thing is bad enough. But then to lie about it is even worse. If only you had told me the truth right away."

"Oh, Oliver, we never, never, never will be so wicked again."

"I have forgiven you. But it is more important for you to ask God to forgive you. When one of His children does a wrong thing, it grieves the heavenly Father very much."

And so it was that two blond heads bowed low that night, learning what it meant to say, "and forgive us our trespasses." The heavenly Father, who is always ready and willing to forgive, that night forgave two little girls who belonged to Him. And peace returned to their hearts.

But it was not until the next day that the girls learned what it meant to say, "as we forgive those who trespass against us."

* * * * *

When Oliver reached home that evening he was met by two sobbing sisters. "*Now* what in the world has happened?" he wanted to know. "Don't tell me you have been naughty again!"

"Oh, not us, Oliver, not us. We've been good as can be. But you just come and see what those nasty cook's children did to our garden."

Oliver felt very sorry when he saw the garden. All the flowers were pulled up by the roots. Everything was ruined. Even the little gate and tiny wheelbarrow were smashed.

29

As he stood there looking at the wrecked garden the same two fat faces appeared in the bushes. "So you will come here where you don't belong?" they yelled. "We told you we didn't want you here. We don't like you. We don't like your garden. And we'll smash it every time you make it. So there!"

The cook's children made the same awful faces at Oliver and the girls and ran up the hill.

"Go after them, Oliver!" Babs yelled. "Go after them and smash their fat faces in for them. We hate them!"

"Yes," Debbie screamed, "we hate you! We hate you!"

Oliver took the girls by the hand and led them back to the cottage. What a lot he had to teach these girls.

That night Oliver talked to them before prayer time. "You found out what it meant to say 'forgive us our trespasses,'" he said. "Now it is time you learn what it means to say, 'as we forgive those who trespass against us.' You wanted me to forgive you when my sketch was destroyed. Now you must be willing to forgive those children who destroyed your garden." But it was a long time before the twins could bow their heads and say *those* words.

"Isn't it funny?" Babs asked. "We've been saying 'as we forgive' for a long time and yet we weren't willing to forgive at all."

"Yes," Debbie answered. "I guess we were using 'vain repetitions.'"

30

The very next day when the fat little faces appeared, Babs called to the children, "Would you like to come and help us in our garden? We'd like to be friends with you. We forgive you for doing what you did yesterday."

"No tricks?" one fat face wanted to know.

Debbie smiled at him. "No tricks," she said.

The girls saw then that the two fat faces belonged to two chubby bodies as the cook's boy and girl came out of the bushes and began to help to rebuild the garden. Soon, however, they tired of the hard work and did not bother the twins again.

CHAPTER SEVEN

"Lead Us Not into Temptation, But Deliver Us from Evil"

One day Babs decided to climb to the top of the wall which separated their garden from the gardens which belonged to the big house. "Oh,

Debbie, you should see how nice their garden looks now." Babs had her trowel in her hand and it fell over the wall.

"Now what will you do?" Debbie wanted to know.

Babs held her finger to her lips. "There is a man coming this way," she said. "I'll just ask him to pick it up for me."

31

"Hello," called the very tall man as he got close to the wall. "Is this a wood elf I see up there?" He handed Babs the trowel and looked over the wall. "And there is another one there—another one just like you."

"We're twins," Babs explained. And before long, because the gentleman asked them many questions, he learned all about them—for the girls loved to talk.

"I don't live here," he said. "But I do come to visit fairly often. I shall hope to see you again. But tell me more about your brother and the paintings you say he does."

"Well, he can't paint as well as Mother. Not yet, that is. He nearly cried when he had to sell Mother's painting. It was the last one she did before she died. And Oliver says it is a picture of the home where she lived when she was a girl."

The tall man was silent for a moment or two. Then, "I wonder . . . Can you tell me where your brother sold the picture?"

When the twins told him, he said, "Then it was I who bought the picture." He walked quickly away leaving the twins staring after him.

When the girls told Oliver about the tall gentleman who had bought their mother's picture, he was interested. But the girls did not know the man's name. "We just called him Mr. Graybeard," they said, "because he has a gray beard. He seemed to like that."

"Well, if he doesn't live in the big house we probably shall never see him again," Oliver said. And promptly forgot about it.

Oliver was often lonesome in the evenings. He had no companions his own age. So when a young man who worked in the bank with Oliver and lived in a room as Oliver did, invited him for supper one evening, Oliver accepted the invitation.

32

When he got to the young man's rooms he found two other fellows there also. After a good supper, cards were brought out and they began to play for money. They took it for granted Oliver would play. Oliver thought, *I cannot be rude after this kindness to me. And they need me to make a game. I'll play tonight. But I won't come back again.*

But Oliver did go back again. The first night, and the second, and the third, he won money. It seemed an easy way to get the things he and the girls needed. So he kept going back.

Soon Oliver began to lose money. He kept trying to win it back again. Finally Oliver owed his friend thirty-five dollars.

Owing the money worried Oliver. He would have to start going straight home and to the hill

to paint sunsets. He knew the paintings would sell.

33

Left alone in the evenings, the twins began to go to the village. They made friends with a woman who kept a candy store. She felt sorry for the girls and allowed them to help her in the store. The landlady did not like for the girls to be out in the evening, but she felt it was not her business. So she said nothing to Oliver about it. The girls would hurry home and get quickly into bed before Oliver got home. Quiet Time Notebooks and prayers were forgotten.

When Oliver arrived home early one evening —meaning to paint—his sisters were gone. They did not get home until after dark.

At first Oliver was inclined to be cross with them. But they looked so surprised and guilty when they saw him, it reminded him of his own guilt. He knew he had neglected them.

"Come, girls, let's go to our rooms," he said quietly.

34

The girls sat on the edge of their bed, frightened by the look on their brother's face. "Do not be afraid," he said gently. "Just tell me everything. Where have you been and what have you been doing? The landlady tells me you have been going out every afternoon and not getting home until dark."

"Well, Oliver, we didn't do any harm—not until tonight."

"Yes? What about tonight?"

"Well, we were helping the candy-store lady to fill bags with candy. And when she turned her back, we each took—stole—a piece of candy. We popped it into our mouths real quick so she didn't see us."

"But we did tell the candy-store lady about it afterwards," Debbie said, "and she wasn't cross. She offered us another piece of candy but we wouldn't take it. We were too ashamed."

"The candy just seemed to stick to our fingers, Oliver. So I guess we'd better not fill candy bags and be tempted anymore."

With a deep sigh Oliver said, "Well I am glad you told the lady and are determined not to let the temptation get the better of you. It does often trip you up before you know where you are. We must be on guard against these temptations, and we'll pray harder than ever, 'lead us not into temptation, but deliver us from evil.' We all need to pray—hard."

Debbie kissed her brother's cheek. "Not you, Oliver," she whispered. "You don't need to. You are always good."

35

Oliver shook his head sadly. "Let's get these notebooks caught up, shall we? I'm sorry I've neglected you so much. Have you been saying your prayers each night?"

Now it was the twins' turn to shake their heads sadly.

"Then let's start again right from the beginning of the Lord's Prayer," he said "and see if we remember what it means so far."

Together they prayed. Then Babs said, "I know sure enough what 'Our Father' means."

"And the 'which art in Heaven'," Debbie volunteered. "Mommy is there. God, too. He takes care of her there and of us here."

"And we know what it means to 'hallow' God's name. We even got Amos, back in the park, to 'hallow.' When we love God—really love Him—we won't have to be reminded not to take His name in vain."

"And when we pray 'Thy kingdom come' we are asking God to hurry and have His kingdom come right here on this earth."

"We're remembering pretty well, aren't we, Oliver?" Debbie asked.

Oliver nodded,"What's next?"he questioned.

"Well I guess we need to pray hard, 'Thy will be done on earth as it is in heaven' so we'll do God's will and not Satan's." Babs looked guilty.

"What next?" Oliver ignored the guilty look. He knew he had not been doing God's will himself.

"Well we certainly know what 'give us this day our daily bread' means, cause we've been getting our daily bread each day."

"And sometimes sweet rolls, too," Debbie added.

"And we learned what it means to forgive others like we want to be forgiven."

Oliver was satisfied that his sisters knew their lessons well. "The next part of the prayer is 'and lead us not into temptation, but deliver us from evil.' Now, if you don't go into town evenings, but stay at home and work on your lessons and on your Quiet Time Notebooks, you won't be so apt to get into evil. The same goes for me. I've been playing with temptation, too. Let us pray again, and really mean it, 'deliver us from evil.' "

"Now we've just got the 'for Thine is the kingdom' part left to understand," Debbie announced.

"And the 'forever and ever,' and the 'Amen,' " added Babs.

A few days later, as Oliver was taking the girls to Miss Gregory's for lessons, they saw a tall man driving a big car. "It's Mr. Graybeard!" the girls screamed together.

CHAPTER EIGHT

"For Thine Is the Kingdom, and the Power, and the Glory, For Ever. Amen."

36

When Mr. Graybeard heard the twins screaming at him, he stopped his car and got out to talk to them. "So this is the brother who paints pictures, is it? I suppose the girls have told you it was I who bought your mother's picture."

"Yes, sir," Oliver answered politely.

When the tall gentleman invited Oliver and the girls to visit him the next week, Oliver accepted gladly. "Everyone is so kind," he said.

"Why did he look and look and look at you so, Oliver?" Babs wondered after the man left.

When the day for their visit arrived, the twins were really excited. "We liked Mr. Graybeard right from the start," they said. "But, Oliver, do you know we still don't know his name? He only told you where he lives, didn't he?"

"Well, if he likes Mr. Graybeard for a name, he probably thought he'd just let it go at that."

They found the big, old-fashioned house. Mr. Graybeard opened the door for them himself.

They ate their meal on a big table set with lovely dishes. The little girls sat up straight and were most mannerly.

Oliver noticed many lovely paintings around the house. But when they sat down to eat he noticed his mother's painting hanging on the wall in front of him. Beneath it hung four of the sketches which Oliver had painted and sold to the man in the shop.

37

Mr. Graybeard noticed Oliver staring at the pictures. "Have you seen any of these before?" he asked.

"I blush to see mine beside my mother's," Oliver replied.

"You like to paint?"

"I *love* it. I wanted to be an artist. I should like to have studied art. But I never had lessons, except from my mother."

"Your mother taught you well. But why have you not studied?"

"It is because we do not have the money," Oliver said simply.

The man looked at Oliver keenly. "Have you no relatives to help you?" he asked.

"I believe we have an uncle somewhere. We came to Topminster to find him. But either he has died or has moved somewhere else.":

"Do you expect him to support you if you find him?"

Oliver held his head high and looked Mr. Graybeard straight in the eyes. "No, sir. I'd never ask him to do that. But he might give me some good advice. I am only fifteen years old, you know."

"But quite a man for all that, I can see," Mr. Graybeard said.

Oliver kept looking longingly and lovingly at his mother's painting.

"Do you know why I bought that?" Mr. Graybeard said.

"I suppose, sir, it was because you liked it."

"That is true. I liked it very much. But it attracted me most because it is a picture of my childhood home."

Oliver stared at him. "But it was my mother's home. Did you live there before, or after my mother?"

"I lived there at the same time your mother did."

"Then you—you are . . . "

"Yes, Oliver, I am your mother's brother. I am your uncle."

38

The twins slid down from their big chairs. They walked around to Mr. Graybeard and put their arms around him. "We just knew our uncle would be a nice man, Oliver. Aren't you glad it is Mr. Graybeard instead of that Mr. Smith whose wife was so mean to you? You see, our Father knew all the time we were going to find Mr. Graybeard—our uncle."

"Your name, please, sir?" Oliver asked, still shocked.

"My name, Oliver, is Smith—J. Smith. But recently I have added another name to mine. It is the name of a great friend who has passed on. I am now known as Mr. John Crawford-Smith. This is why you failed to find me, I think.

"It was while I was visiting my friend in the big house, close to you, that I met your little sisters. I fell in love with them. They reminded me of my sister when she was small. And when they told me their story, I was sure you were my sister's children."

"We are so glad we have found you, Uncle," the girls said timidly. "We would have picked Mr. Graybeard anytime for our uncle. Now to think you are really he." Four little arms went tighter about Mr. Graybeard's neck. Soon they were all crying a little. And none was ashamed of the tears.

When the little girls went out into the garden to play, Oliver and his newly found uncle had a long, serious talk. Oliver told his uncle as much as he could remember about his mother. He told him all that had happened to them since their mother died. He left nothing out. He even told about his gambling and the money he had lost.

The uncle soon saw what a fine nephew he had found and before Oliver and the girls left for their home, everything had been arranged for them to move into their uncle's house where the girls could have proper schooling and Oliver could study art.

That night, Oliver and the girls felt they already knew what was meant by, "for Thine is the kingdom, and the power, and the glory." Even though God's kingdom was not on this earth as yet, He did rule and He made everything come out right for His children. Surely they had seen some of His power and His glory in their lives.

39

Together Oliver and the girls did their Quiet Time Notebooks. Then, after prayer, Oliver said, "Just see what God has done for us because we trusted Him. Surely His is the power and the glory, as the Lord's Prayer says. Our biggest troubles have turned out for our good. Remember how bad we felt when we were turned out of our place in Topminster?"

The girls nodded, remembering the wrong things they had done there.

"Well, if we hadn't been sent away from there, we never would have come here and probably would never have found our uncle. And when I took my picture to Mrs. Sutherland and found she was away, I was disappointed, because she would have paid me more than the man could in the shop."

"And if you were rich you would not have sold the picture and our uncle would not have bought it. So it was good we were poor," Babs volunteered.

"Yes, and if you had sold it to Mrs. Sutherland our uncle would never have even seen it," Debbie said.

Oliver smiled at his two happy sisters. "Since you are both such good thinkers," he said, "perhaps you can understand this: Our Father in heaven is the King. But He is absent for a time. Someday He will come back to this earth and this will truly be His kingdom. And so we pray 'Thy kingdom come.' "

"We knew that before, Oliver," Babs said.

"All right. Now then, even though God is not here as an earthly King—not yet, that is—His unseen power is really ruling. This is His kingdom and we are His subjects. We belong to Him. And, best of all, His power and glory will be forever and ever. We must do whatever He wants us to do. Sometimes it looks as if Satan is having *his* way here. But the power is not really his. It is our Father's power. We must never forget this."

"I guess we understand a little better now, Oliver," Babs said.

"Yes, all but the 'Amen.' How about that, Oliver?" Debbie wanted to know.

"Well, 'Amen' means 'so be it.' If you want all these things to be as you pray, you say 'Amen—so be it,' at the end."

It was Babs who said, "Then I guess we'd better be careful how we pray—pray our own prayers, I mean, not just the 'Our Father,' huh, Oliver? We might pray for the wrong thing and it wouldn't be best for us, even if we thought so when we were praying."

"I'm always going to say 'Amen, if it's Your will," Debbie said.

"I guess that's a good way." Oliver smiled at his sisters.

"I think that will be the best way to pray," he said, "but right now let us pray together the prayer the Lord Jesus gave to His disciples."

"He gave it to us too, huh, Oliver?"

"Surely. He gave it for all who believe in Him and are His children. Let us pray, thinking of the words and really meaning everything we say. Then we won't be doing what the Lord Jesus said *not* to do—we'll not be using 'vain repetitions.' "

40

With a new life stretching before them, Oliver and the twins knelt together, never to forget the many lessons they had learned through their study of the Lord's Prayer. Sincerely and earnestly they prayed together:

"Our Father which art in heaven, hallowed by Thy name. Thy kingdom come. Thy will be done in earth, as it is in heaven. Give us this day our daily bread. And forgive us our trespasses, as we forgive those who trespass against us. And lead us not into temptation, but deliver us from evil: for Thine is the kingdom, and the power, and the glory, for ever. Amen."